MIDLIFE ACTION FIGURE

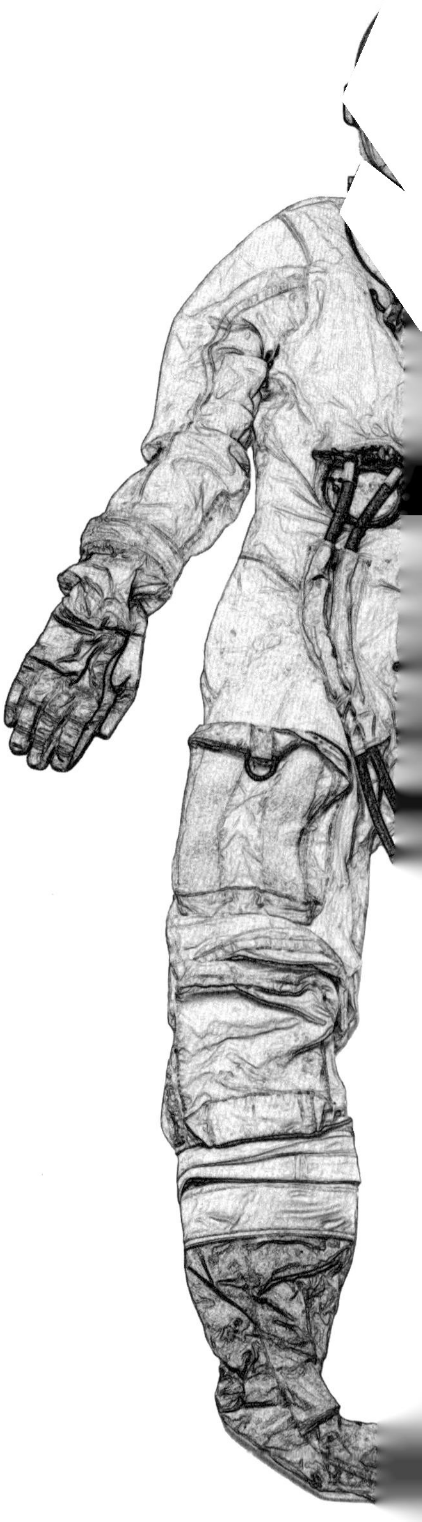

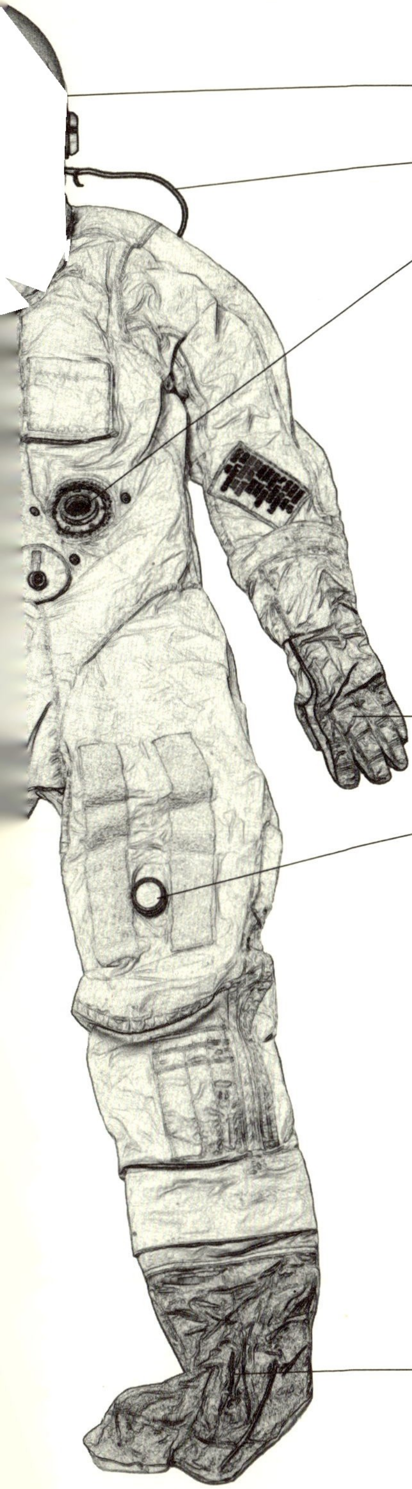

MIDLIFE ACTION FIGURE

CHRIS BANKS

POEMS

ECW
A MISFIT BOOK

Published by ECW Press
665 Gerrard Street East
Toronto, Ontario, Canada, M4M 1Y2
416-694-3348 / info@ecwpress.com

MISFIT

Editor for the Press: Michael Holmes/
a misFit Book
Cover design: Rachel Ironstone
Cover image: © Central Intelligence
Agency / public domain
Author photo: © Jay Parson

LIBRARY AND ARCHIVES CANADA CATALOGUING IN PUBLICATION

Title: Midlife action figure : poems / Chris Banks.

Names: Banks, Chris, 1970– author.

Identifiers: Canadiana (print) 20190109793
Canadiana (ebook) 20190109823

ISBN 9781770415058 (softcover)
ISBN 9781773054100 (PDF)
ISBN 9781773054094 (ePUB)

Classification: LCC PS8553.A564 M53 2019
DDC C811/.6—DC23

The publication of *Midlife Action Figure* has been generously supported by the Canada Council for the Arts which last year invested $153 million to bring the arts to Canadians throughout the country and is funded in part by the Government of Canada. *Nous remercions le Conseil des arts du Canada de son soutien. L'an dernier, le Conseil a investi 153 millions de dollars pour mettre de l'art dans la vie des Canadiennes et des Canadiens de tout le pays. Ce livre est financé en partie par le gouvernement du Canada.* We acknowledge the support of the Ontario Arts Council (OAC), an agency of the Government of Ontario, which last year funded 1,737 individual artists and 1,095 organizations in 223 communities across Ontario for a total of $52.1 million. We also acknowledge the contribution of the Government of Ontario through the Ontario Book Publishing Tax Credit, and through Ontario Creates for the marketing of this book.

ONTARIO CREATES

ONTARIO ARTS COUNCIL
CONSEIL DES ARTS DE L'ONTARIO
an Ontario government agency
un organisme du gouvernement de l'Ontario

Canada Council for the Arts
Conseil des Arts du Canada
Canada

PRINTED AND BOUND IN CANADA

PRINTING: COACH HOUSE 5 4 3 2 1

This book is for Hannah and Noah

Poetry is an act of mischief.

— THEODORE ROETHKE

CONTENTS

ONE

TWO

THREE

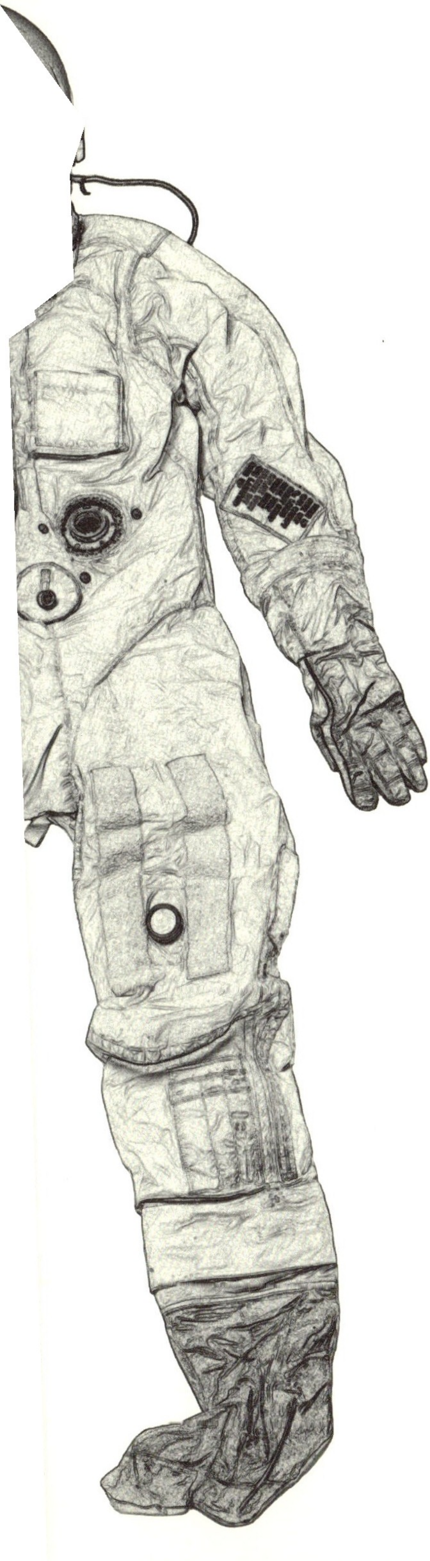

ONE

Time's Atlas

Some people treat each day like IKEA instructions.
Others look for a higher dimension in church pews.
Hot yoga studios. Time is an atlas. A Fisher-Price
View-Master of first kisses and "no return" policies.
I wish this were even more poetic. Throw in the phrase
in medias res like a trial balloon. A benediction. A spark plug.
Another celebrity has overdosed on booze and benzos.
Every story deserves a splashy two-page spread. Despite
Old Navy ads and toothpaste for sensitive teeth, the heart is
a scourge. My spirit guide is a scarecrow. The first-person
singular feels wrong here, but the hive mind, all that buzzing,
overwhelms me. How many different ways to say *Hallelujah*?
I think we would all feel better if we were allowed to fall apart
one day out of the year. If only we could burn the briefcases.
I miss the sound of cicadas. Electric dusk. What do they care
about the end of post-modernism? Birth of narrow-casting?
Everyone has a few words they would like to bury forever.
I am losing landmarks as I get older, but thankfully we can
google it all. The little white house on a hill overlooking
the highway needs a new coat of paint but it is still there.
The uranium mine, the miners, are gone. If you feel yourself
going crazy, you probably are. Only a little. Young men
in black and white photographs, wearing soldier uniforms
or baseball attire, stare out stoically from the back wall
of dimly lit bars and taverns. Today, wellness programs
preach resiliency like they are selling hamburgers. I keep
turning the pages of time's atlas. I trace its illustrations
with my fingers. The contoured lines. The last pages
blank, then something, new shapes, a lost continent,
new ports of call. A secret harbour, or a penal colony.
I mark a big X where the future will make landfall.

Museum of Failures

Henry Ford's first two automobile companies failed
before America fell in love with the Model T. Cold
Fusion would be a great name for a nightclub,
or a game engine. In the Museum of Failures, uniformed
men panic as the *Hindenburg* bursts its small nova,
a piñata of fire, over a naval airfield in New Jersey.
Sky cars and jetpacks never make it past design.
Frankenstein's monster is fiction, unless, of course,
it is a metaphor for a viable pig-human embryo,
or nuclear deregulation. Chernobyl and Fukushima
are no one's holiday destinations. A husband awakes
in restraints on a hospital gurney after deciding to go
for one beer. Another military operation goes horribly
wrong. In the Museum of Failures, there is a whole wing
dedicated to the human heart, its ability to self-detonate,
cause catastrophic loss. The story of the body is failure
amid evolution. Success is an algorithm sifted from many
defeats. Our lives are a landscape of small failures, but
we love to look at photo albums anyways. My inner
life fails to meet my expectations. Let's stop pretending.
Be our authentic selves. Let's stop failing to hear one
another. I've always wanted to write a poem called
"The Caretaker of Loneliness Meets a Young Courtesan,"
which is either brilliant or a terrible title. Be honest,
but not too much. Emotions are okay, but keep out
the bodily fluids, unless it is blood. In the Museum
of Failures, this poem is written on a parchment of skin,
kept under glass, beside Creationism and the *Avro Arrow*,
adult baby food and vegetable-flavoured Jell-O.
If you are reading this, know you have failed to remain
undetected. The authorities are coming for you.

Ivory Towers

Burn the canon. Didn't we do that last year?
Spread ashes on the seasons. The oak tree is
an anthology of leaves. No one is yelling at it.
Tell me one true thing and I will regurgitate
shadows. I was a failure in academia. Ivory
towers trigger my fear of heights. Never coat
an enemy's shirt in poison ivy when you can
rub his face in it. I redact that last statement
for fear it will be used against me. Degrees
wash up onto a beach like stranded jellyfish.
Poems are devotional candles. Stop praying
to yourself. I wish I understood a second
language so I could get tenure. I hope you
are reading this with white gloves in a library
full of mahogany desks, brass lamps,
green shades, red tomes, austere bookshelves.
Alas, archives are for staff members only.
The librarian says you can keep that little
magnifying glass as a souvenir as long as you
don't set fire to the building. First editions
are restored, gently put behind glass doors,
sold at auction. Even if I take the stairs, two
at a time, I will never make it to the top
in this lifetime. Often when picnicking in
a field or walking my dog, I see the towers
in the distance. Cloaked figures standing on
balconies either in need of rescue, or in silent
contemplation. It makes me a little jealous.
The ascent is arduous and full of *coup d'états*.
Imagine that view. A kingdom of one.

Witnesses

Popular culture is in remission. Some people
are watched like chronic illnesses. I wait for
the next market crash, hip youth revolution,
measles outbreak. I'll take three wishes please.
Then maybe three more . . . Don't think about
other centuries too much, or your life will be
disappointing. Depression is running amongst
bulls, or Chinese water torture. Our anxiety
comes in thirty-one flavours. A prosecutor goes
off his meds. He is no good to us. You win
the case on your own, or not. Note: the weather
never asks for help. The government wants more
of that DIY attitude. Memories are orphans.
Do you want Darjeeling tea, or chemotherapy?
How many would like a choice? I miss poets
who have died. Their poems stick around,
witnesses telling the truth of what they know,
but eventually most of us stop listening. Start
networking. You have been contracted to bear
this bundle another day. To suffer fashions
until the prognosis changes. I wear being
like an ill-fitting coat with a few buttons missing.
How long has it been since you played marbles,
or kissed a relative stranger? Keep pitching ideas
until one hooks, starts tugging. Something will
emerge from the briny deep. Be yourself, they say,
which has something to do with a gate closing,
a hardship post, the self a ghost haunting a tower,
an upper walkway. Make your peace with it.

Stolen Matches

Existence is not for the weak. Consciousness
moves like a river beneath sheet ice. I make
going to the grocery store an event. Every meal
when you are single is a sad banquet. So what
if we are incisors, daydreams. Hey Muse, hit me up.
Let's go dancing. The lyric makes its little noise,
something like, *out of the darkling sky come*
the white stars, little frozen glyphs, or Valkyries
burning in separate Valhallas. No more hand-me-downs.
I have nothing up my sleeves except nerves
forming a small city with dirty cabs. I don't
want to learn the patter, the schtick, of one word
against another. I want the feast. The offal
I leave on a silver dish for gods who
starve this time of year. Choose wisely
amongst the coloured rags. Memorize
traumas. The after-life is a recital. Hello loss.
Hello exaltation. Have I made you smile yet?
Know this poem is a forgery. I traced it by hand
in elegant calligraphic script. Like a dry drunk,
I want more and more of what I cannot have.
Emotions disfigure perception. Open all the doors.
What is the difference? Heave-ho the familiar
and see what takes its place. The scope is cavernous
so take a good flashlight. I follow my thoughts
into a gully where they are playing with stolen matches.
Isn't that always the case? Put away the Play-Doh
when you are done. The school closed down years ago.
Clean up the art tables. I'll lock up after you.

Queue

Take a number and hold my place in line.
Spend twenty-five years of life asleep.
Three months in traffic. Forty-eight days
having sex. Cut out the part about bears
feasting at a town dump. Hornets haunting
a summer camp. Stop being a hostage
to the quotidian. Ever hold a megaphone
up to a flower? Wear sadness in a lapel?
Your memoirs are burning. I struggled
to retrieve them from the fire. Some words
are glowing. Others turn to ash. Walk me
through the *mise en scène*. Connect the dots
so the story includes a few minor themes.
Hope amid devastation. Alter egos and
slices of birthday cake. You are tempted
to step out of line for a moment. Realize
when you fail to return, no one notices.
It is best to put the past on shuffle. I retain
rights to my pain and my designer clothes.
The rest is yours: eleven years working.
Fourteen days kissing. Two years watching
commercials. When they finally call out
my number, I'll be ready for my close-up.

Tom Swift

I have a minor crush on Saturn's moons. Callisto,
Io, and Titan. The rent is too high. I read once
about a boy inventor who built rocket ships. Dark
forces, mysterious agents, always conspired
against him. Leaving the planet for the vacuum
of space was an easy decision. Meanwhile,
the first time you are hurt in love you discover
the body is a spacesuit with a lifetime supply
of oxygen. Floating untethered leaves you gasping,
Come back to me, you say. Those words
bleed through to the suit's interior, where you
feel trapped. Try to make it to the ship's bridge.
I built model rockets as a kid. Launched them
from a yellow field. I never intended to vacate
this world. NASA says they have found exoplanets
in outer systems that can support life. Still, no
nude beaches in space. No Comic-Cons, foie gras,
or walk-in clinics either. As you get older, you feel
the pull of gravity more. Dreams less. On the way
home from school one day, you notice you are being
followed. Your father is a brilliant scientist. Why
has he been kidnapped? Taken to a secret moon base?
You head for a launch pad. Your rocket is waiting.

Gulag

Guilt is everyone's personal gulag. Don't think so?
Read your lost letters. I once told a girl I hated her
with the white hot intensity of a thousand suns.
Another girl I cheated on with my roommate. Guilt
is the body's dark canvas. How many joules does it take
to say sorry? I wouldn't know. The spirit holds
a public hearing. It calls itself to testify over and over.
Maybe we can become better people. I'm trying
to be sincere. A song is mounting. Let's hold
hands. Wait for our bodies to blossom. Whenever
a woman's face fills with grief, I can't stand it. Turn
off the camera. I'm on the brink of tears. The bees
are emptying hives. Stroke my cheek. Who assigned
me this life? To educate one's emotions is not
a work of genius. It's the blood's heritage. We rub
perceptions against one another, sometimes even
bodies, hoping for a revelation or two, to drown
out the Muzak. To live with those faces staring back
at us from the mirrors of mall lavatories. We hurt
people. We love people. How else to say it? Tomorrow
calls you sweetheart. Don't waste it. Get out of
the way of happiness. A blessing. We should be like
children in kindergarten, all smiles and group hugs,
our emotions transparent, joy's helium carrying us
lightly across a playground, if we are to see others,
have them see us. But what about guilt, you say?
Its patina stains the soul. Wasn't Paradise the story
of its birth? A garden once immense and undamaged.
Tell that to the children and I will have no choice
but to walk out of here, leave you cold and alone.

Green Spider Tattoo

What is the procedure for when friends die
and you need to manipulate words? Divest
yourself of secrets. I knew a guy who nearly
died working a chainsaw from a treetop.
One minute he is pruning a largish branch,
and the next, he misses the artery in his leg
by a half-inch. Some people are just lucky,
I guess. It's all scratch-card wins, bilateral
symmetry, and evolutionary fitness. Beauty
is an advert for good genes. How does it
do it? I mean nature. All that math. X and Y
chromosomes. Some three billion DNA
bases the same in most people. It sounds
tiring. Gaia sitting there, with her internal
calculator going all the time, not paying
attention to what the kids are doing. One
opens a soup kitchen. Another vandalizes
the post office, stealing all the Christmas
card money and social security cheques.
How many kids can you fit in the back
of a police car? Seven. When your father
is a police officer, he does a puppet show
in front of your class in grade three. Then
chaperones all your dances in high school.
He whispers the sins of a man walking
on a sidewalk in your ear as you drive home
together one day. It is like being God.
I look at my students and the wreckage
inside them is hidden. One boy I taught
killed another boy with a machete. I wish
I made that up. He had a green spider tattoo
on the back of his neck. I wish it forever.

Simulation

Beauty rewrites its own code. The authentic
is another souvenir most people throw away.
I have lived over seventeen thousand days
waiting for this latest round of beta-tests
to be over. I want the gold edition. Here,
let me hug you. Maybe push the hair from
your face. There is no better model
of human connection. I desperately want
the real, but there is a subscription charge
if you want to message. The evening rain
has stopped. There is another possibility:
I am lying to you. Swipe right anyways.
Every time you breathe out words, they die
at the moment of their hearing. Says
who? We need a backup plan. I remember
something, and a little Xerox copy of me
appears mowing a lawn, meets up with friends,
takes back a neighbourhood street from a rival
group of kids. Some people believe
we are living in a computer simulation.
No wonder it feels like I am going nowhere
half the time. Are we only digital puppets?
Evolution and my own heartburn says no.
If yes, the turkey vultures circling the edges
of the suburbs are a nice effect. Already
I feel less lonely and isolated knowing
we are part of the same program. Let's
share secrets, fall in love, blow big shining
bubbles in the artificial sunshine before
some god sitting at a desk propped up
by a couple of milk cartons, a wizened face
searching a screen, hits control-alt-delete.

Reading So-and-So's Selected Poems in a Used Bookstore

I like the jade dragons and the bougainvillea.
The various mistresses of Paul Klee, Gustav Klimt.
Jackson Pollock pissing in a fireplace at a party.
A locomotive hauling away a sibling's death.
Allusions to Pompeii. A Greek philosopher du jour.
A token villanelle. An amusement park.
Roller coasters on fire. What beautiful rhymes!
Afro and gazpacho. Crocus and hocus-pocus.
Syllabics of beauty and despair and truth
hidden in musty stacks. Someone's handwritten
notes in the margins: *Love this one! Huzzah!*
Haikus solemn as frogs beneath a lily-white moon.
Lyrics a reminder of the shadow's dark roost.
How about this one poem with sledgehammers?
A grand piano overflowing with Blue Morphos?
A Japanese actress who cut off her lover's genitals,
threw them into the sea? The last poem
in the collection will rip your heart out, I swear.
It's about a boy throwing rocks at a seagull,
smashing its wings. The bird hopping broken.
The Gatha of Atonement. Its little prayer.
Human shame like a shipwreck in a bottle.
The poet's photograph is in black and white.
He lives in a French chalet, or as a recluse
on a Greek island, summers when not teaching
freshman about poetry and personal failure.
There is an Ivy League campus in the photo's
background. His crow's feet, grim smile, say
each day, I walk out of my French chalet, or
a white house with a blue door, heading
to the old town, poems gestating, where I buy
my breakfast, a newspaper, thinking about
friends back home. At night, in my dreams,
I put a contract out on this poet's life.

Scrapbook

Here are old ticket stubs and pressed flowers.
A picture of me with punk-rock red hair. A guitar
I played four hours a day for years. This is me
at my first teaching job. A girl is doing henna
on a friend's forearm. She leaves thirty *Don't Do*
Drugs stickers all over the classroom. This is me
picking at the soft glue of my adult life. Here is
the boutonnière I wore to a Sadie Hawkins dance.
Life Savers, a white doily, coloured streamers.
Here are years of trying to drink myself invisible.
Can you see me? Me too. Here is a black eye,
a bloodied face. My grandmother breaking a hip,
then me running to the neighbour's next door.
Here are all the precious moments time forges
stuffed into a dossier, a scrapbook of worries,
the evidence misfiled, or tampered with, so you
have to sort it yourself. The pages are dust
and moonbeams. Lightning storms and yellow grass.
I have left places for new pictures. Absences are
intentional. There is one of a polar bear to show
my grandchildren. One of me at a demonstration.
I am reading poetry, or some kind of manifesto.
You can tell by the blue flames kindled in my eyes
I believe defending ideas is worth a little tear gas
and riot police. Let's all fight for a cause, even
if that cause is getting out of bed in the morning,
pasting down pictures, and using up all the glitter.
I bequeath you these pages instead of an *Ars Poetica*.
Add anything you like. A butterfly conservatory.
Tiger Swallowtails, Ulysses, beauty's useless wings.

Thunderdome

It's not easy, Dear Reader, to be
locked in a cage match with you.
Stand on my shoulders. Stare out
the narrow casement of chance.
I think we got off to a bad start
when you caught me in bed
with your past and a bevy of vowels.
Look, I'm proud of you the way
you polish the bronze telescope
of these words, expecting to see
size D elegies, ambrosia martinis,
red carpet origins, a sadness gala,
beyond my clowning, jumping up
and down. Sorry I keep moving,
crossing from my side of the page
to give you sugar and angel porn.
I like it best when we forget each
other, accidentally touch. I am
a glacier melting at the speed of
memories leaving you. It is hard
to say what it is we want from
a relationship. We forget birthdays.
This should not be a tug o' war.
We shout friend or foe endlessly
across a patch of no man's land
even though we have matching
passports. You take the window seat.
The view I am told is spectacular.

The Beggar

I had been working twenty years in the same office
when I found I was short of change. Someone had
bought doughnuts, and we were all to pitch in. I asked
a coworker for fifty cents. He immediately gave it
to me. I looked at the money in my hands, rubbing
my thumb over the Queen's heads. It made me think
of all the days coming into the office. The stacks
of paperwork I shifted from my desk to my manager's
desk. Who would sign the pink forms in triplicate
if I were to quit? "Thank you," I said to the office
secretary. "I will be taking an indefinite leave
of absence." I began to remove my tie and jacket.
A group of people circled me near the glass wall
entrance. A woman in a pencil skirt gave me a hug.
My manager said I was making a grave mistake.
I gave my red sports car away to an intern in a blue
cardigan. I told her it was due for a tire rotation.
I headed outside and walked to a busy intersection.
I undid the first three buttons of my shirt, took off
my socks and shoes. I rolled up my sleeves, sat
against a light post. Another man was holding up
a cardboard sign that said, *Homeless. Need money
for food*. He said, "Buzz off, this is my corner." I told
him he could have the keys to my house. He did
a double take and then said, "Really?" I told him
it was a brick one and half storey on a nice little
cul-de-sac in the suburbs of the city. I gave him
my office business card and told him to report
to my manager. That a job had just opened up.
"You might wish to shave and shower first.
There are fresh clothes in a bedroom closet."
He had tears in his eyes when he shook my hand.
He asked how could he ever repay me. "Can
I have your sign?" I asked. He handed it to me

before walking away. That was weeks ago. Most passersby do not pay the least attention to my sign. I eat very poorly. My hair has grown unruly. This is my corner. Believe me, I will defend it.

The Book of the Dead for Dummies

I am past my best-before date. Some would argue
water is not a human right. Maybe we are all dead,
awaiting rebirth. I do not believe the world exists.
The universe is a giant hologram. Any first death
is a practice run. We are stranded together amongst
the office towers and traffic cops and billboards.
Commuters read popular novels. Stare out windows
on the subway awaiting resurrection. I wish I had
been a better person in a previous life. Miracles
go unseen. Bombs explode on prime-time news.
I am stuck in a holding pattern. Past life regressions
are incarnations to prepare you for the other side.
What kind of prison is this with its plastic water
bottles and big box stores? I am plotting escape.
Let me begin again. I fall asleep every night, only
to wake in the same place. Is it wrong to love
the feast if the guests are all ghosts? I am bound
for a certain term to think about online profiles
and the spirit's inferno. Purgatory is a late shift.
Experience is an illusion. Had I grown up with
demon gods, I might have been reborn already.
I treat everyone like emissaries of the hereafter.
Heart attacks are the way some people transition.
Over time it occurs to me my body is a reliquary
of stardust and unyielding losses, and despite my love
of calla lilies, the smell of aftershave, massage
therapy and hotel pedicures, Arabica coffee
and French baguettes, morning smoothies and air travel,
as an astral plane, I give this one three stars.

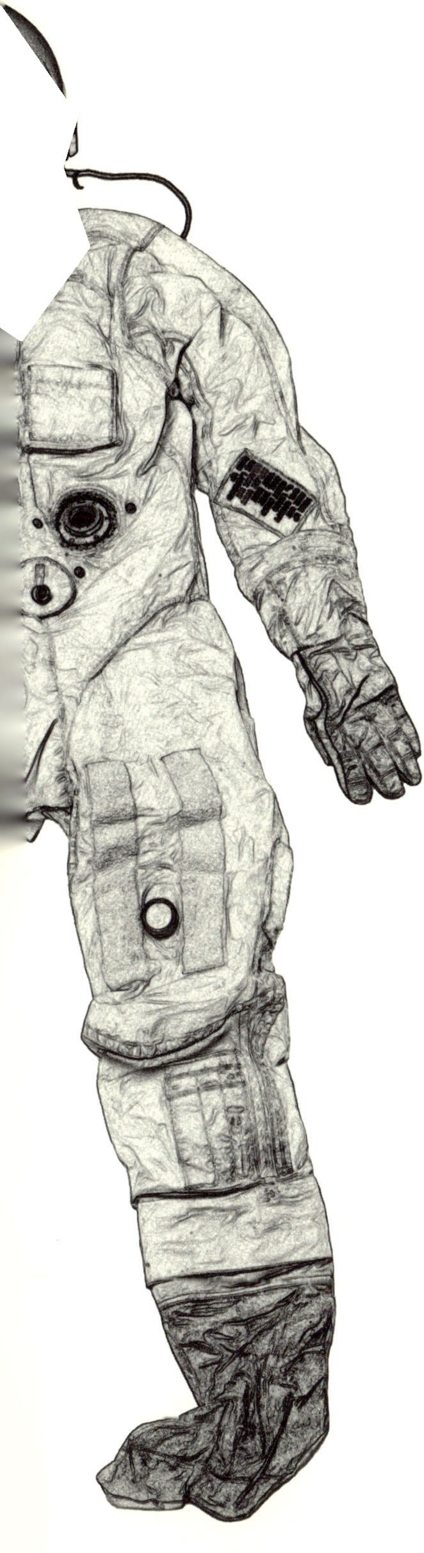

TWO

Honesty

I know nothing about lightness, or the inner
landscape of beauty, or the divining rod of truth,
or any other risible poetic statement. I have not
pressed eternity into the palm of my hand,
or stood in the possession of visions. Most days
writing a poem is like watching a pot waiting
to be filled. You get up, pull on your pants.
If you are lucky, images streak across your brain
like a meteor shower. The best poems make
Matryoshka dolls out of time and feelings
and memories. They talk about the ancient world,
or the soul's rusted-out streetcar marooned
in a farmer's fallow field. This is an honest
poem, and even it is on the grift. It mentions
the Rosetta stone, a Latin prayer *Deo gratias*,
a collapsed diamond mine lost in the night,
a cavern full of cool spring water to sip from,
a key to musty catacombs, a phantom radio
playing songs from adolescence, a paper rifle
taking aim on a grassy knoll, a mouth speaking
secrets in a foreign tongue. Maybe the poem
is just putting us on. It talks behind our backs
to its friends. I would walk away but already
the poem has spun us to the top of a Ferris
wheel, and there is nothing to do but sway
in the night breeze, waiting for some mechanism
to grind forward. To haul us back down to Earth.

The Interview

Ignore the other applicants sitting in cages. How badly
do you want this job? The pay is lousy and the office
needs you to reconcile disparate things. What can you
do with this vase of flowers? This shadow creeping
across a desk? Our business is remaking the world
so we need real go-getters such as yourself who can
make a black reef of umbrellas appear at a funeral.
Dark hymns of rain fall at the stroke of a pen. Or
the opposite, the sun's asterisk of hope to punctuate
a worthless day. We need you to embody the past.
To learn forgetfulness as a trade secret. There is
a bright future for you once you understand every day
you are dying a little. Are you taking notes?
There are only a few last questions. What was it like
when your grandparents died? Are you seeing a therapist?
Tell us about the invisible world. Edvard Munch
or Willem de Kooning? Do you like being naked?
Have you ever had real absinthe? Would you say you
are more of a burning effigy or an aurora borealis
person? Name five shades of blue. Explain the Magna
Carta. Other than the ocean, what sounds echo inside
a seashell? What illusions do you cling to? Whisper
your one true lover's name. Do you exist? One final
disclaimer: the last two applicants burnt out after only
two weeks. All their friends had become strangers.
You may be tempted to leave too if you hear whispering
through the walls. Some voices are real. Some not.
Here are the keys to the entrance. Don't worry if I am
not back in the morning. Let me gather my things.

The Good Samaritan

May I give you a tour of the past's haunted house?
Thieves picked my pockets clean but I can help you
with the secret origins of the ego. I have an X-ray
detailing its emptiness. I can build a fire with only
a few brittle verbs. Show me where it hurts. Here
is a map of the village of your childhood. Let me
lead you through its narrow streets and alleyways.
Once I was not helpful. I stayed alone in my house.
I said no to anyone who came by talking of money
or proselytizing. All that was folly. May I chauffeur
you around? Do your grocery shopping? Be your
personal saviour? Please, allow me to do my part.
Let me be a surrogate for your pain and loneliness.
Here is some cotton candy, and all the addresses
of everyone you have ever loved. I can make calls
emphasizing how sorry you are if you wish. It
really is no trouble. Might I suggest a hot springs,
a back rub, a turn-of-the-century Russian novel
to make you feel less like a clod of earth? We all
do bad things to each other. I hope I am not
keeping you from some pressing appointment?
Give me five dollars, and the name of the boy
who hit you in grade five. I'll take care of it.
If you are addicted to abandonment, let me
hold your hand while you sweat out any aches
from under a blanket. Your restraining order
did appear a little gauche. I'm doing this for you.
Where are you going? I'll pick up the bill.

Threat Detector

A boy in my son's kindergarten class has been
diagnosed with lymphoma. They told the kids
he has gone to a new school when really he is
in a hospital attached to machines. Chevrons
of geese are flying north way too early this year.
Gold stocks are rising but pennies are dwindling.
A friend was attacked getting off a bus by a total
stranger. I thread my keys through my knuckles
when walking alone downtown at night. The pills
I take for acid reflux may cause kidney failure ten
years from now. Another city is contemplating a new
landfill in my city's backyard. I worry my children
will not love me as they get older. Cougars attack
joggers on hiking trails. Another politician was
caught in a lie. A scientist is gagged. Klaxons blare
every time I visit a dentist. Brain cells depreciate
over years. Revoke the names of musicians, artists,
actors I once had access to. Hundreds of pilot
whales are beaching themselves in New Zealand
and Cape Breton. I should be counting blessings,
not character flaws. The forecast for tomorrow
is a nimbus of anxieties and more subterfuge.
Lockdown drills are commonplace at my work.
If a tornado comes, I will be in the corridor
holding a candle. Music was better thirty years
ago. Code Red. Code Blue. Too many codes
and passwords. The ozone hole is bigger
than North America. My son thinks his friend
has moved away. He wants to wave goodbye.

New World

A ship arrives in the middle of a downtown city
intersection. Although there is no port, people
depart the wooden ship with family belongings
stuffed into suitcases, saying, "So this is the New
World. Who knew it would take this long to arrive?"
Men and women walk past them on sidewalks,
staring into phones, cursing some inner lack.
The newly disembarked hold hands, begin to sing
a hymn forbidden in the land of their ancestry.
All around them, skyscrapers reflect clouds, loom
above the assembled crowd. At once, a policeman
tells them to move along, or he will ticket them
for an unlawful assembly. Where are your permits?
Children hide in the long skirts of young mothers
caressing their golden hair. Was this the land they left
the old country to find? Their leaders urge caution.
Maybe they should reboard the ship for the night?
But the captain has pulled up the gangplank. The ship
is sailing away without them. Evening draws its veil
as a kettle of people tightens around the newcomers.
They begin to chant. Assimilate! Assimilate!

Lay Believers of the Metaphysical

The world keeps talking shit, spreading havoc,
seismic quandaries, everyone quarantined in separate
bodies, forced to share a native language, fathers
and sons, mothers and daughters, how lonely
this movie is, its chorus of ash and salt, the word
happiness a pebble in our mouths, what we cannot
swallow, and yet nothing will break it. It's a mystery
to have gotten this far, every step blinder than
the last, courthouses full, psych wards overflowing
with teens, and yet daybreak with its secret knock
sometimes wakes us into new understandings, enough
to drag the mechanisms of our muscles out of bed,
to forget the scars and dark wounds experience
opens and cauterizes in an endless cycle. Moments
are dress rehearsals. Hold the applause. I harbour
the nameless and try to drag it out into the light.
We, lay believers of the metaphysical, need a raise
before we are all out of a job. Self-knowledge is on
furlough. The ersatz is appraised. Raven or dove?
It changes the prophecy. Don't bother answering
the door. It's just the unseeable playing ding-dong
ditch. The miniscule and the large are truant. Ruffle
their glitzy pages. Master or apprentice? Depends
on which hall of mirrors. The tickertape says you lost
the whole sum. The zodiac is as useful a clock as any.
May I take up five minutes of your time? I have
this brochure and a message of grave importance.
Ignore the cardinal's red flame bashing itself against
the window. It's not a symbol of living or dying.
Keep this one fallen feather if only to be sure.

Garnish

Check out these invisible handcuffs. Death
is classically trained. You are free to go
on your own recognizance until the time
of your execution. Every minute is garnish.
The entrée is missing. We live under
an embarrassment of stars. Each face
is a living portrait. A work in progress.
Dreams build cantilevered balconies into
the world. Hold this mirror. So begins
our secret congress. Let's not meet
out in the open. What do you wish to know?
I promise to pull you out of an earthquake.
Give you first aid. When the ocean recedes,
do not go walking amongst the fish gasping
in its wake. Head for the hills. Stay with me
one more week. Wave goodbye before
slipping into a dark limo filled with techno
and champagne. I hate the crowds so I won't
be at the premiere with its paparazzi. I'll be
working on my patents. There is this one
for a new type of glass. When you hold
a hand up on either side, it simulates human
contact. Here, place your fingers like this.
I forgot how warm you are to the touch.

Living Will

To a lifetime of self-loathing, I leave this
god-hunger. To the girl I held in my arms
in the middle of winter, her boozy breath
warm against my neck, her form skipping
home through the falling snow, I leave
my scarf of regrets. To my brother who
shares my disease, a tumbler of ice and
promises. To my friends, a collection of
books and the dust of my envy. To my
father who picked me up from a police
station when I was eighteen, my face soft
with bruises, as I screamed at the room
of assembled officers, *Why don't you hit*
me some more? I leave this pail of guilt.
To summers at overnight camp, I leave
vespers of friendship. To the bully who
wiped his nose on my shirt, I leave a suit
of bees. To loneliness, a drought of days.
To sex, peeling away each desire, I leave
our separateness. The hard candy center
that cannot be licked away. To television
news, I leave this picture of a serial killer.
To the forgotten celebrity, disappearing
marquees. To decades of work, an elegy
of no consequence. To my ego, this one
Wallace Stevens poem. To my children,
I leave my crown and a survival manual.
To anger, I leave this hairpin storm. To
perspective, these contact lenses. To my
many students, I leave this mid-term test.
To my teachers, a shrapnel of right words.
To my critics, the movement of beads
back and forth on the abacus of taste. To
the river, I leave a tackle of lost lures and

weeds full of fish. To emperors, nothing.
To the field brightening with yellow flowers,
I leave a little red fox in possession of you.

Jade Pendant

I have a slow leak. Think of a bike tire
made of being, slowly deflating itself.
I walk through my house, and I start
dropping things: Neptune's 900 mile
an hour winds, Caravaggio's *Medusa*,
the fact 100 lightning bolts hit the Earth
every second. The names of Eastern
deities, a graffiti mural on the side
of a boxcar, Cesare Pavese's interior
monologues, a piece of rose quartz
I found as big as my fist. Truths
and half-truths. I try to pick them up.
All the nights I got drunk and didn't
remember what happened. That time
a homeless woman with a torn coat
called me a stinking sexual criminal
as I crossed a street. Maybe my brain
needs to declutter, so forgets the names
of movies I cried through. And movies
I wanted to see. With every inhalation,
a sad refrain whispers, *Let me out.* I feel
things spilling out of me like an art gallery
modelled after an insect's compound eye
I never built. Hymns I sang in church,
which tasted like vinegar. The seven ages
of man. A jade pendant bought at the foot
of the Great Wall. Names of boys I made
run away from school. A comic collection.
If you insist on staying, grab a basket. Look
carefully. Help yourself to anything of use.

The Laboratory of Aesthetics

For some people it's massive city bridges,
Woody Allen movies, strawberry-decalled
teapots, German WWII paraphernalia.
Others thrill at a Brillo box in a museum,
Gerhard Richter's overpainted photos,
or Radiohead's *Kid A*. There is always
that one guy willing to explain French
New Wave. How *Breathless* is the best
movie ever made, and not because of
the cool sunglasses, when really it is
the cigarettes and the cool sunglasses.
I have to admit France never looked
so good. Take an object, cast it in silver,
blow it up about two hundred times
its normal size, set it up in a public square,
and I guarantee people will take selfies
around it. The laboratory of aesthetics
these days is really about mischief
and surprise. For instance, I was writing
another poem about Buddha and panic
attacks, but aesthetics dictate I throw
myself off the deep end. So now there
is a Californian subdivision engulfed
in wildfires, and the state is all out
of water. A riddle without a satisfactory
ending. I don't get it? You are going to
fit right in, says Buddha, whom I tried
to keep out of the discussion. Let's just
say aesthetics is irony taking the piss out
of everything, which is why you should
rummage through culture's junk drawer
and pick your favourites from the mess.
You may not understand why you love
the things you do, like Jack Gilbert's poems,

scarab beetle collections, wood turned boxes,
the 1974 Ford XB Falcon, a Diane Arbus
retrospective, her mesmerizing photograph
of a boy with a toy grenade, his face squeezed
into a grimace, but they understand you.

Subject Matter

Better a talking parrot than a cello unchaperoned
on a stage. Better an Aztec Empire than a kingdom
of Kodak moments. Never mention tarot cards or
dark tunnels. Take an image and enter through
the fire escape, the back window. The front door
has too much foot traffic. Rifle through old family
stories but upset no one. A teen runaway has left
his group home with a suitcase. Is he going to his
grandmother's house or his dealer's apartment?
A man surrenders his gun in the middle of winter.
He and his wife were sitting around the dining table
of the old farmhouse when their son came home
from university with a boyfriend. He weeps in the back
of a police car apologizing to the police, hoping
the son he just disowned will feed the exotic birds
he raises in his barn. Plumage his one passion.
Childhood might be a matchstick house, or a rusty
swing set in a vacant lot, the whole apparatus rocking
a little if you swing too high. Keep out the mortgages
and gift cards and self-help gurus if you can. Death
is better as a bored teenager in a red usher uniform,
flashlight in hand, than a black-cowled bony figure.
No psychologists or laugh tracks. The poem is allowed
to keep name-dropping old classmates, secret crushes,
icebergs, Mexican painters, the sky's stretched canvas.
Happiness is too precise a word. So is sorrow. Sandblast
their syllables and start again. Hell is a blank page. Read
back my notes. These rules are meant to be broken.

Romance

I never understood it. The candy and chocolates.
The rose petal path leading to a boudoir or hot
bath. Not that I am an ungrateful lover but a circle
pendant meant to symbolize love or union loses
meaning over time. Know only I hold myself out
to you the way a young black cat holds a snake
in its jaws, alive and wriggling, the feline purring
as it offers its gift proudly to a squeamish owner
at a back screen door. Know I would cut through
a barbwire border to make my escape with you.
Save you from a witch's oven in a house made
of gingerbread, chimney forged of red licorice.
Know I would break radio contact, orbit around
the dark side of the moon, if it would be the only
way to bring me back to you. Heights make me
dizzy but I would stand at the mountain's summit
just to hold your hand. Throw my transparent net
around the trees near midnight if only to capture
your pain there. I would stoke a wood stove, pull
the quilt of our shared years up to your chin. Wrest
hope from shadows, sit in the sidecar of an Italian
motorcycle if you were the one driving. Oppose
despots if they took you as a political prisoner.
Light a votive candle, and pray to the saint of us.
Know the tape recorder is on, and I fully testify
although I do not yet know your name, my cold
devotion is only to you. My passport to where?
Not a place, never a place, but a flush of feeling,
this breathing carving our initials into the air.

Notices

The rain is past due. No one need go to court
if you answer the summons. All the people
you hurt while growing into a man are now seeking
damages. Next time, bury the bodies a little
deeper. Someone cannibalized a lyric poem.
They found your fingerprints and a hippopotamus
at the scene of the crime. Jury duty sounds
slightly more fun than three days of DTs.
Stay away from the woman smoking Gauloises
cigarettes. She will try to bribe you with similes,
spiritual illuminations. The hydro company
is threatening to cut power to the orphanage.
All those children wasting away in the dark.
You have been accepted to a fake seminary,
offered admissions to warring poetic schools,
been drafted into an army. Sign the contract
or you'll never understand a river at twilight.
The disclaimer reads: the rewards are real
but the contest is rigged. The zoning office says
your neighbours are planning on expanding the yard.
They built a trebuchet and now have proper
permits for its use. Doctors warn tests revealed
a malignancy. You will die slowly over the course
of a natural lifespan. It is a bag of spun gold, or
your first-born by month's end, writes someone
at the collection agency. This is the last notice.
Make arrangements. Your credit score rates
higher than your mental health index. Write off
the difference. The bank will give you an extension
on your next midlife crisis. Bills must be paid.
No, you cannot use dark matter or Stonehenge
as collateral. Your reserve funds will last you
two weeks. I'll write you a bad cheque.

Say-So

The buzz-buzz of commerce. Robots are coming
for our jobs. A tech apocalypse without
laser guns or a rugged organized resistance.
Who wrote the song "Will You Still Love Me
Tomorrow?" I strike my flinty *I* against
the world and watch the sparks fly. Each
memory is a gravestone. A piece of driftwood.
Our fears are democracies. The gatecrashers
will inherit the parties. Until they are over.
Never ceasing is the secret to a long life.
I'd rather rest my head against the anvil
of uncertainty than the Bible's yada yada yada.
There is a lake of fire or fluffy white clouds
inside every person. I'm sorry but I cannot
nullify my thinking. Will you be my darling?
Here, I brought you this bouquet of birth
and hardship and death. Hit refresh.
Set your imagination to self-navigate.
The bridges are out. Satellites keep transmitting
your location to the rich and powerful.
No more prefab houses or dime-store metaphors.
Remnants of the Big Bang pixellate
the universe. Always an ache at the edge
of something. Redraw the borders.
When the shutters blow open, let the seasons in —
it's so easy to surrender one's say-so.

Crusade

No one wants the good china. Meet me
at the safe house. Pry up a few floorboards
and you are sure to find an old beer bottle.
Who wants my head on a platter? Pencil in
time for friends and enemies. The billet-doux
was lost in the move. Life is not packed
in Styrofoam. I'll take a riot over the ho-hum.
Devastation over racquetball. I will sign
your petition if you will sign mine. Change
should not require forms. My resentments
come in transcripts. Joys in hot pink neon.
Do you want the egg-salad or the gospel?
Own up to your hurts. My style is foreign
so the heart suffers. Obligations possess me
until I feel like a rolled-up tube of glue.
How did I get stuck in this meat locker?
At least, I have Dante and Beyoncé to keep
me company. Careers are scams. I am waiting
for the next great crusade. Let it be sharing
our inner lives. Tapestries of secrets. The
past declassified, and still parts omitted.
Who needs to be a prisoner of blue skies?
Ante up on hope, and I will double down
on happiness. Fly your banners. I give you
my assurance of a promised march over lands
full of payday loans, corporate retreats. Let me
put my armour on. This takes several years.

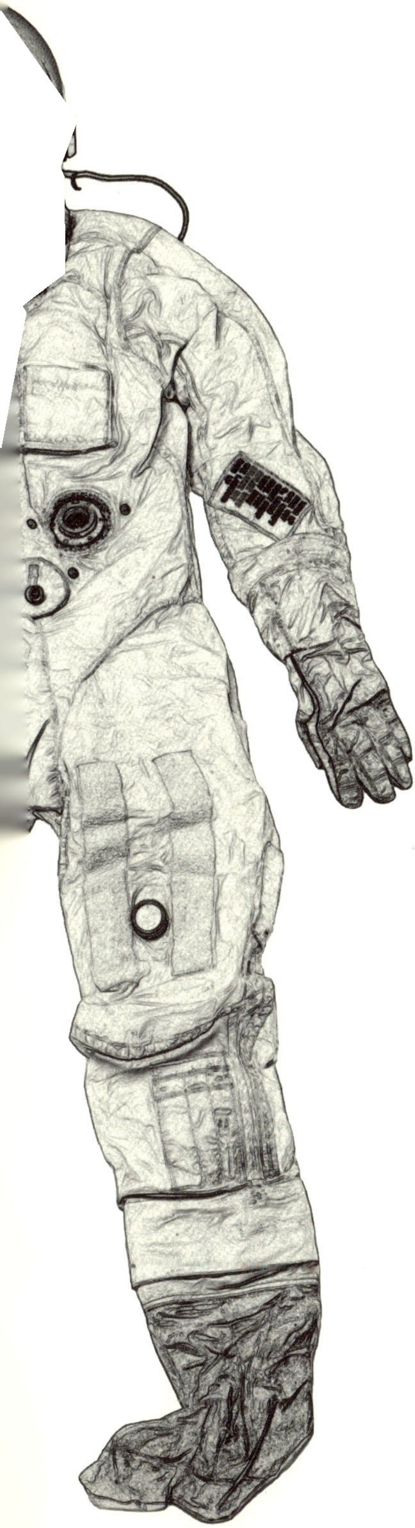

THREE

Big Questions

Every child will tell you the big questions
are what is your favourite colour or how
old are you? Existence an *amuse bouche*,
not a Tommy gun firing into the dark.
Words are totems. Remember wisdom
sprang from the head of a god. Questions
change with the decades, like how many
blackbirds flew out of that pie? Do ghosts
sleep? Why is there no thirteenth floor?
Will I get the credit, the job, the apartment,
yes or no? What is your sign? Myers-Briggs
type? Fred Astaire or Ginger Rogers? Lou
Reed or David Bowie? How many attended
the wedding? The divorce? To tweet or
not to tweet? Should I jiggle beauty's lock
using only a paper clip? Does this skirt go
with my ennui? This tie with my exhaustion?
Should I be worried I no longer get ID'd
at restaurants? Twenty years on, why keep
making art? Swag or sparks? Is this puppy
show-quality or rescue? How do I love thee?
Does a honeycomb of doubts or assertions
produce a sweeter honey? A vale of soul-
making or a glen of happy sleepwalkers?
Who jinxed me? cries last year's prom queen
storming from the gymnasium. Air or water?
ponders the amphibian its entire life.
The big questions expand like black holes
and we, hovering on their event horizon,
rush toward them at the speed of light.

Emergency Broadcast System

The emergency is happening. Hide the Monets
and bottles of Lafite. Please exit the building
in an orderly fashion. We interrupt scheduled
programming to say public safety has been
breached. The emergency sits in our blind spot
so no changing lanes. Order the coq au vin
and crème brûlée for it will be your last meal.
The conservatory is on fire. Please remain calm.
Authorities have been notified. They refuse
to go down with the ship. Write a letter to an old
university flame. Take a hatchet to your insecurities.
Start an argument with the moon. This message
will repeat every sixty seconds. Think of it
as a ritual. Make a circle in the middle of a room
linking arms, facing outwards, with children
on the inside. The emergency goes unchallenged.
There will be no discounts. Stop torturing
yourself by appearing normal. Empty cash
registers and cages full of laboratory animals.
Listen for foghorns. The emergency refuses
to be categorized as a natural disaster, a financial
meltdown, or a spiritual bankruptcy. Put on a kimono.
Worry your forehead with fingertips. Tell yourself
you were not an accomplice to the current crisis.
I have a confession to make. This is not a recording.
The broadcast is inside you. What is your favourite
song? It will play next. The emergency is over
the moment you understand spiders on ceilings
have nothing to do with doomsday. Take a few
deep breaths. Your survival depends on it.

History

Imagine years with serial numbers
ground off in the hands of ancestors.
An assassin kills an archduke.
A pyramid is built in honour of
a mediocre ruler. A double agent
walks twenty miles through enemy
territory to warn of an impending
attack. Brown shirts goose-step
through city streets and no one
is laughing anymore. History
takes it in calmly. Interviews
witnesses. Reconstructs a scene
from a few clay pots and ruined
adobe walls. A stone altar
and a pit full of skulls. History says,
Don't eat the pickled herring,
or go boating during a storm
off the Gulf of La Spezia. Sometimes
history cannot solve the crime. This
results in a hung jury. The script
is Minoan but untranslatable.
A sea captain returns to an island
but all members of the colony
have disappeared. A marriage
sails into a port of call but no one
is on-board and the captain's log
is missing. History fails to make
sense of what happened. How did it
capsize? The past without a curfew.
No wonder History is panning for gold.
A few shiny grains is all we ever get.

Vacation

It was an island of people arriving and departing.
Musicians played exquisite wooden drums
and strummed guitars. Heaps of fruit trays sat
on white banquet tables in the middle of a stone
courtyard. A local man wearing a floral shirt
handed us an exotic cocktail. "Here," he said.
"Drink this potion." A chef was cooking
suckling pig over an open fire. The guests
could smell the ocean, but were told to stay
off the beach at night. Feral cats sat in trees
like otherworldly sentinels. The many faces
blended together like the chords of a song
in a foreign language. "Tonight, you are rulers
of the world," said our gracious host and, at once,
dancers appeared, scattering little lizards across
the courtyard. My female companion whispered,
"This music, the dancers, the cocktails, it's all
a kind of blindfold, isn't it?" A shirtless man began
eating fire. Cheers went through the crowd.
"We are a congregation without eyes," I said,
listening to the wind in the palms. I watched
the faces of a couple dragging suitcases toward
a checkout. No angel at their backs. Only time
pressing them forward, their pockets emptied,
the striptease of paradise already at an end.

Twenty-First Century Self-Portrait

It takes a village of robots and explosions
to raise a summer blockbuster these days.
No alms for artists. I am allergic to most
sequels. There should be a special victims
unit for poetry students. My entourage
dried up with the Canada Council money.
Crank the air conditioning and dopamine.
Gone are the times when you could write
eloquently about blueberry bushes.
Troy is forever burning, and yet all we do
is shop online. Why did we stop going
to the moon? Brochures for space tourism
should be flaunting the moon's artisanal
emptiness. Every year I get older and my
heart grows an extra ring. The alpha guys
who drove trucks and played hockey
in high school are dead from heart attacks,
or have cancer. Details matter when you
are overseeing air traffic or working
your way through the beads of a rosary.
The air after rain smells like a mixture
of green and iron. The miraculous sends
everyone into a panic like a fire alarm
at midnight. We are approaching a dead end.
Rats are growing immune to our poisons.
Elephants are born without tusks to spite
poachers. How are we evolving? Without
any reverse. Tears of sadness, tears of joy,
look different under a microscope. Well,
after all these decades, doesn't everything?

Elegy or New Deal

The fallout zone is closed for holidays.
Upper management wants to sign hope
to a three-year deal worth all the stars
breathing a trillion sighs of relief. Tell me
to be more authentic and I will leave you
standing alone at a chapel. Tie up regrets.
Leave them by the back door. Rest on
laurels, or sweep them into green piles
in the yard. Recalibrate the imagination.
Check the glossary of the unsaid. Stranger,
our trial separation has been a complete
success! Take off our masks. Reinvent
astonishment. My best thinking has led me
here at your behest. I'm not qualified
to mix different chemicals, only words.
Besides, my lab partner is sick and all
the labels have peeled off. Don't run
your finger along the edges of this life
unless you like to taste your own blood.
Any gainsaying is purely coincidental
but the forms still need to be filled out.

Conversation

"I want to build a compound on a mountaintop,"
says one friend. "The federal government is always
burning down mountain compounds," says my best
friend sitting next to me. "It gives their emergency
response teams something to do." All of us sigh
heavily. "Besides," says another, "what would you
do on top of a mountain? Go fishing? Collect guns?
Hate on groups of people?" The first friend giggles.
"No, I think I would just wait for someone to come
wandering up my mountain," he says, "then share
what little I have with them." He smiles at us
as if acknowledging his naïveté. "That never works,"
says my best friend. "Everyone is, at first, sharing
chores, and then the next thing you know two people
are fighting over the good sandals. Or the cute blond
who shows up with only a backpack on a Wednesday."
"Yeah, but you can really see stars on a mountain,"
says the first friend. Another in our group who has
been silent to this point speaks up. "The stars would
make everyone feel small and vulnerable. A wish to
connect with a higher power would begin to grow in
everyone." "Is that so bad?" asks my best friend.
"It is if one in the group begins spouting Bible verses
and claiming to be a prophet," says my quiet friend,
shaking his head and staring at his shoes. "It is all
hymns and campfires and 'Kumbaya' for the first
couple of years, but eventually everyone is drinking
poison Kool-Aid." "No Kool-Aid on a mountaintop,"
someone offers. "Why do we do this?" says my best
friend. "Plunge the knife into each other's dreams?"
"Because it is easier than building a compound
on a mountaintop," says my first friend.

Merry-Go-Round

The search and rescue party ran out of champagne.
Let's toast our disengagement! So what if seabirds'
bellies are full of plastic, and the world's storehouse
of seeds, secured in the high Arctic, has been ruined
due to the permafrost melting. Is Mars really Plan B?
Self-talk is a voodoo doll. Earth is a plague of sky-rises
and smart monkeys. More labyrinths, fewer scars please.
The human brain is just an elaborate compass so why
is my head still spinning? I want to kiss more strangers
though I still believe in monogamy. Cynicism is very
fashion-forward this season. I need a matching tote
or caddy for my feelings. My Wikipedia entry should
read: Here lies one whose name is writ in HTML. Yes,
the world is dysfunctional but just go with it for now.
Even the philosophers don't understand themselves
anymore. So much art is just wallpaper for small cafés
and dive bars but who would have it any other way?
We are each doled out a certain portion of meaning,
different from each other, which is why some call
others infidels, and why it is exciting to meet those
who share the same sexual portfolios as we do.
Oh Horatio, tell my story and share my Instagram!
My tragic flaw is telling jokes about death. Biographers
keep asking me to slay more dragons. I say start with
mysterious origins and childhood signs. Let us test
clairvoyancy. Guess what I am thinking? The psychic
fairgrounds has closed for renovations. Hop the fence,
stand beside me until you hear words, my thoughts,
whisper between booths. Our stars are crossed, but
our fortunes are the same. I want to ride the steel
merry-go-round with you. That feeling of spinning
and spinning, then flying off the face of the Earth.

The School

Tired of being a student? Start a school.
Carve a path. Woo acolytes with honey.
Tell them you will teach them all about
beauty and strangeness. Write for thirty
years. Snare an angel. Nail its wings
to a barn door. A river is a correspondence
course. All my masters are dead. Throw
away the manuals. Stoke the mysteries.
I will build a new school on the prairies.
A parcel of land with cattle and buffalo.
Some mountains in the background. We
will write in the mornings, sing praises
while holding hands, strolling the green
wheat, in the afternoons. People from
a neighbouring school, one built beyond
the low foothills, will stop by wanting
to share stories. How nice it would be
to accept their offers of friendship! But
the school needs protecting in its infancy.
We tell the strangers to wait for us down
by the creek, the one large willow, while
we grab ivory-handled knives. We do what
must be done, then bathe in the waters,
until our hands are clean, evening tamed,
the sun crimson as the blood we shed.

Midlife Action Figure

My body feels made by Mattel.
There is no lifetime achievement
award for surviving emotional
trauma. Van Gogh cut off an ear,
went about his day. I don't mean
to make light of suffering. My alma
mater tells me by phone they could
be doing better. Can I coat-check
this malaise? Talking to neighbours
feels like treading water. Similes
are passé. I need an electrician to
rewire my mood. Going to parties
when you don't drink is open-heart
surgery without anesthetic.
I've completed all seven seasons
but my knees are arthritic, and
my chakras are in shambles. I love
how business thinks innovation
is dreamt up in hotel bars and
conference rooms. Being forced
to take the arts package is what kills
creative embryos. My depression
is pure Suzuki method. I'm going
to open a Montessori school
for recovering addicts. Ever seen
a masterpiece wrapped in cellophane?
Go to your local record store,
dig around in the stacks. Maybe
the letter does not arrive on time
so you drink poison, or decide
to take up pole dancing. Either way,
someone's parents end up crying.
Pull the string protruding from my back.
Listen to what I am about to tell you.
There is not much time.

Master Narrative

after Bob Hicok

It begins with an invisible movie title, at birth,
starring you. Then walking barefoot through
sharp grass and dandelion moons. Then
building forts in someone else's forest.
Then the trees stop speaking to you. Then you
get a driver's licence. Then you get a tattoo
you will regret in twenty years. Then the terror
of love. Ecstasy, not a drug, but a feeling.
Chemical elevators going up to the brain's
top floor. A penthouse with shag carpeting
and a heart-shaped bed. Then you shatter.
People look at you like you have fallen down
a hole, as if you are very far away. Then
you climb out of a briar patch of razor wire
in your heart. Then the world welcomes you.
Then you say *grass*, *wind*, *night*, *silence*,
but what you mean is *holy*. A word dissolving
on your tongue like a host, a wafer of Communion,
which it is. Then you walk more carefully
fearing to be broken. Then you attach
a microphone to your shirt in case you say
anything wise. Then you walk to the beach
but the waves speak another language. Then
you bury the microphone which is when
the messages start pouring in. Who's there?
Then you compile all your hours walking
this Earth into a pile of kindling and douse
it with kerosene. Then you strike a match.
Burning brightly like a pyre of troubles
on dark shores is the only way to exist.

Geocaching as Spectator Sport

The coordinates of the past led here. Poetry
geocaches beauty and leaves a trail of words
to follow. Memory is a self-replicating virus.
A fever of images. A havoc of he said, she said.
An armoire of reverence. The soul staring out
between freshly ironed shirts. It needs more
Vitamin D. A mother to push it out the door
saying, Don't come home until the streetlights
turn on! Well, the streetlights have turned on
and the roller rinks have closed down. I grow
older to no great avail. Past loves and hatreds
make nests in me. There are hungry mouths
to feed. To make sense of a sunrise, or a divorce,
or the Ghost of Cast Parties Past is all I have.
I believe in art the way some people believe
in religion. I stand in an altarless place waiting
for the silence to shout back. I believe in
probiotics, and Philip Levine, and my children.
I believe in Terry Gilliam and Missy Elliott.
Gwendolyn MacEwen, and warlords, and free
democracies without party balloons. Sappho,
unfortunately, is not paying my mortgage.
Neither are the pyramids. Everyone needs
kindnesses to exist so I built my own. How
I love the teenage girls giggling, sending texts
to a pack of boys sitting across from them
at the mall food court. The man standing
idly by, near the sushi hut, while his wife
tries on bras at La Senza. The security guard
sharing a joke with a custodian at a drinking
fountain. Our lives are consensual even
though we take from each other. Even though
more could be given. I like these pictures
the ink fills. This framework of locked and

unlocked doors. It passes the time. Put enough moments together and you get a century. I will not live that long but very few do. My absence I leave here. These are the coordinates.

Common Myths

I was assigned these twelve labours,
one of which is to stand in a grocery
line behind the old woman counting
out change and coupons for a lifetime
without murdering anyone. To read
the parable of weather every morning
before picking up an umbrella. To hold
the day's inventory for ransom without
knowing any of its contents. To see
my father's face in the mirror, knowing
we are versions of each other. To fail
at being anyone's hero. To be like you
and not like you. To go steady with
depression, suffering the sad looks
of family and friends. To know we are
only electrons dreaming, and still try
to make one's livelihood. To not argue
about the impossibilities of heaven.
To resist hell. To be on hold forever,
which is how I know the world is not
perfect. If given the choice, I would
start my quests in the middle. I would
stop thinking of my heart as a grenade.
I would learn to be special to even
one person. I would lull the monsters
to sleep. I would be foolish without
embarrassment. I would reap the rewards
of my efforts. I would let the axe fall
upon the unseen. I would be the axe.

Oasis

I thought about eternity until God turned up
dead in a textbook. Capitalism wears its tuxedo over
a blood-stained T-shirt. I like genius al dente.
Jean-Michel Basquiat paintings. His sneakers
scuffing the canvas. I wander this intermission
between TED Talks and the apocalypse. I am
obligated to tell you my sadness is a private desert,
but I'm willing to make room for a small oasis.
Halo or aura? My migraines are real. The world
is a chrysalis full of oil spills and hiccups and missing
children, and yet, something is materializing . . .
All new monuments come in primary colours.
My voice is bronzed. Being brainwashed sounds
like a nice vacation, but how I would miss out
on all this not knowing anything! Anger
can be turned into a hammer if held too long.
A memory is a precious stone. Try not to hit
one with the other. The emitting sound
emanates through decades. Hurts your children.
Your children's children. The play is over.
You sift the narrative. Someone was in love,
then wasn't. Someone gained some valuable
knowledge, then died. The actors stand around
waiting for you to leave the building. If given
a choice, I suppose I would take a waterfall
over Xanax. Beauty demands fealty. Sometimes
you have to close your eyes and fire all flares.

Kintsugi

Your choices go unremedied. If only
we could repair the cracks in one's life
using gold. Scintillas of precious metal
celebrating the struggle. The Japanese
do this with pottery. It feels sometimes
like we are suffering an epidemic
of indifference. Despite our little screens,
it is possible to see one another. I am
the one standing beside sunflowers,
or in the ad for unyielding desire. I am
drinking beer on a rooftop in Old
Montreal with friends while at a loft
party below someone gets famously
drunk, takes off her dress. The past
is what we remember, but also what is
diminishing in other rooms. The salt
in our blood seasons our aches. My
needs are infinite. I wish I could tell
you I am the only one in this poem.
I have taken your pulse. All right, stop
pretending you are not there. The
universe keeps racing in all directions
like nostalgia. Love's velocity. Light
years of trial and error. Already these
lines are exposing the cracks between
a boy on a rooftop in the middle of
winter, and a man who treats his hours
like a waiting room. But what lovely
streaks of gold! The sum of our worth.

ACKNOWLEDGEMENTS

Earlier versions of some of the poems in this book have appeared in the following journals, magazines, and blogs:

Taddle Creek: "The Book of the Dead for Dummies"

Train: a print journal: "Ivory Towers"

Train (blog): "Museum of Failures"

The Week Shall Inherit the Verse: "Garnish"

I would also like to thank Carleton Wilson, Autumn Getty, Aura Hertzog, Jim Johnstone, Stuart Ross, and Paul Vermeersch for their guidance and friendship, which is worth more to me than they know. Lastly, I would like to thank my editor, Michael Holmes; copy editor, Emily Schultz; and all the staff at ECW Press, who are always a pleasure to work with on a book.

CHRIS BANKS is the author of four previous poetry collections. His first full-length collection, *Bonfires*, was awarded the Jack Chalmers Award for poetry by the Canadian Authors Association in 2004. *Bonfires* was also a finalist for the Gerald Lampert Memorial Award for best first book of poetry in Canada. His poetry has appeared in *The New Quarterly, Arc Magazine, The Antigonish Review, Event, The Malahat Review,* and *Prism International*, among other publications. He lives and writes in Waterloo, Ontario.